INTO THE
DEEP

**Life through the depths
of the ocean**
Dr. Mark Norman
and David Paul

wild dog

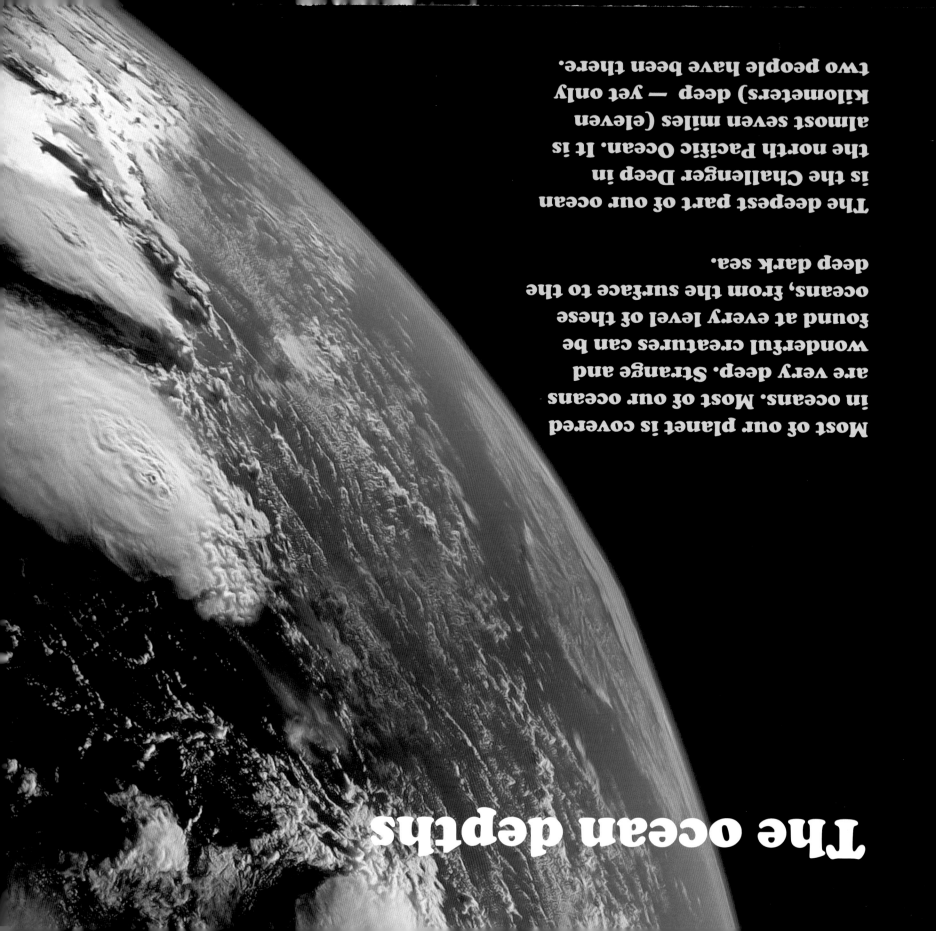

Most of our planet is covered in oceans. Most of our oceans are very deep. Strange and wonderful creatures can be found at every level of these oceans, from the surface to the deep dark sea.

The deepest part of our ocean is the Challenger Deep in the north Pacific Ocean. It is almost seven miles (eleven kilometers) deep — yet only two people have been there.

The ocean depths

In 1960, Jacques Piccard and Don Walsh climbed into a steel ball on the underside of a submarine, the *Trieste*, and spent five hours sinking down.

The water pressure at the bottom of the Challenger Deep is so great, it would be the same as about 50 elephants piled up on your head! More people have wandered around on the moon than have been to the deepest part of our oceans.

Hanging at the top

Some animals live by clinging to the surface of the water.

Bluebottle jellyfish
Bluebottle jellyfish float using an air bubble like a piece of blown-up chewing gum. Their tentacles can stretch up to 60 feet (20 meters) long!

By-the-wind sailor
The by-the-wind sailor is a jellyfish with a sail — the wind pushes it along above the water, while its tentacles catch food floating just below the surface.

Violet snail
The violet snail stays at the surface by blowing a big bubble of snot and air and hanging off it. If it lets go it will sink all the way to the bottom of the ocean. It eats by-the-wind sailors.

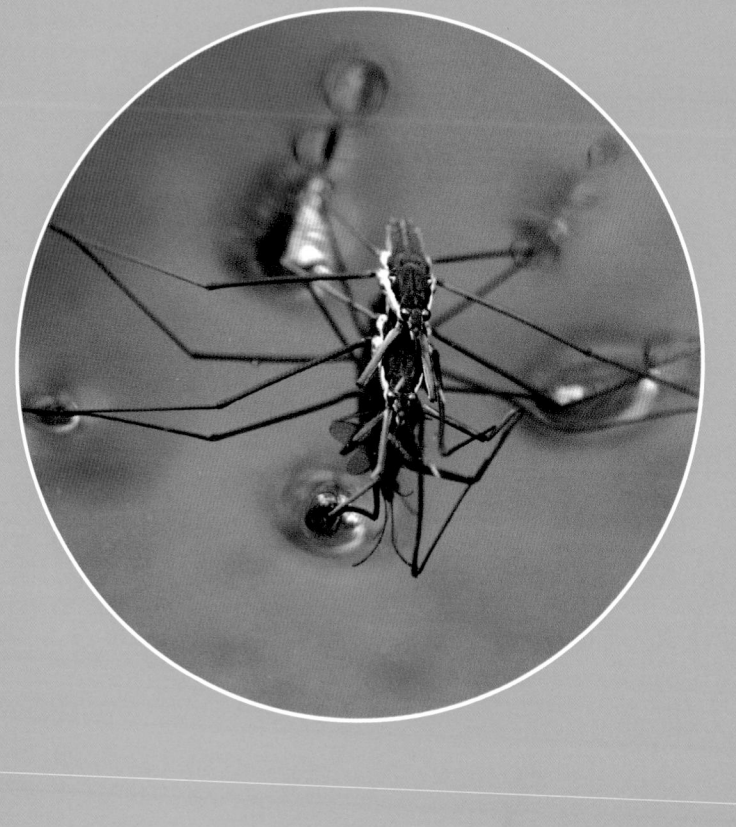

Water striders

There are even insects in the middle of the open ocean. Water striders run across the surface on special hairy feet.

Sea lizard

The sea lizard is a tiny slug that sticks to the sea surface and eats jellyfish for dinner.

Hunting near the surface

There are fast hunters in surface waters, always on the lookout for a meal.

6ft/
2m

At this depth it is now too deep for most people to stand up.

Sailfish
Sailfish use the big fin along the top of their body to round up schools of smaller fish. They then hit and stun the fish with their thin bill before eating them.

Blue sharks
Blue sharks are long, thin, and fast.
Their blue skin matches the blue
water near the surface, so they are
camouflaged from their **prey.**

Ocean wanderers

Many animals cruise the upper layers of the oceans — some drift around for their whole lives, while some are on their way to other places.

A three-story house would reach from here to the surface.

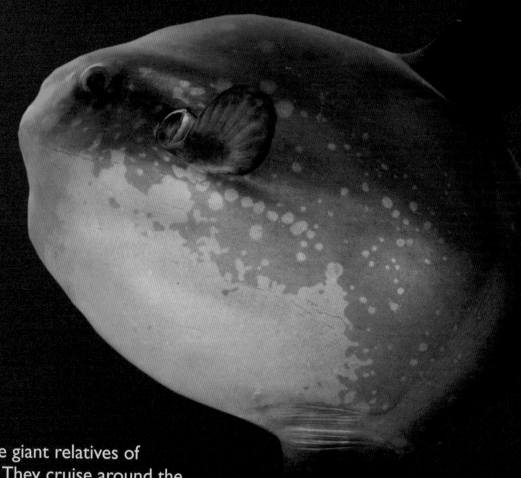

Sunfish
Sunfish are giant relatives of pufferfish. They cruise around the open oceans feeding on jellyfish.

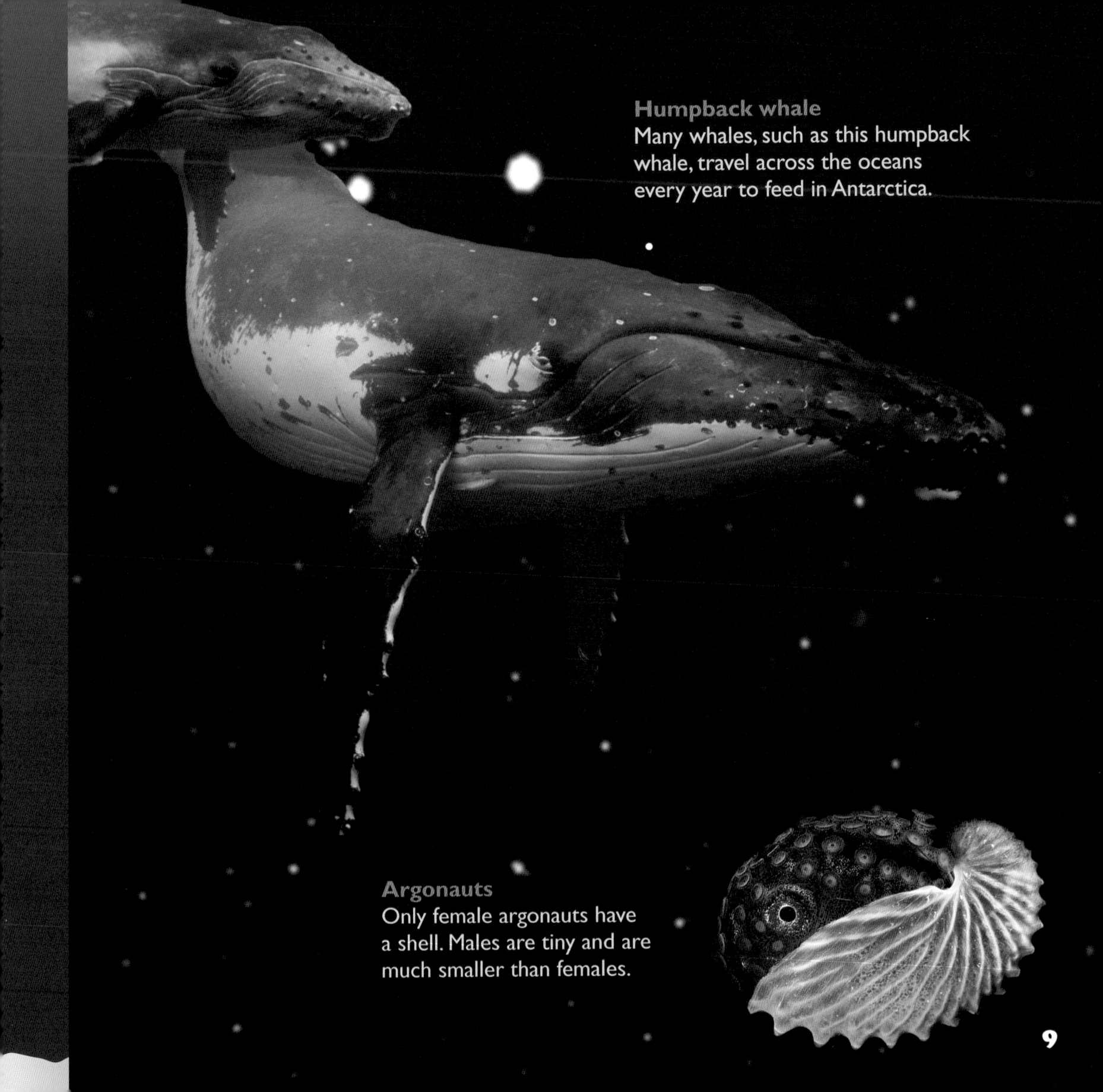

Humpback whale
Many whales, such as this humpback whale, travel across the oceans every year to feed in Antarctica.

Argonauts
Only female argonauts have a shell. Males are tiny and are much smaller than females.

Floating babies

The young of many sea creatures begin their lives floating in the ocean as plankton.

60ft/
18m

Only the best snorkelers can dive this deep on one breath.

Baby octopus
Baby octopuses jet around by squirting water out of their funnel.

Baby shrimp
Baby shrimp have lots of antennae and hairs that detect the vibrations of **predators**.

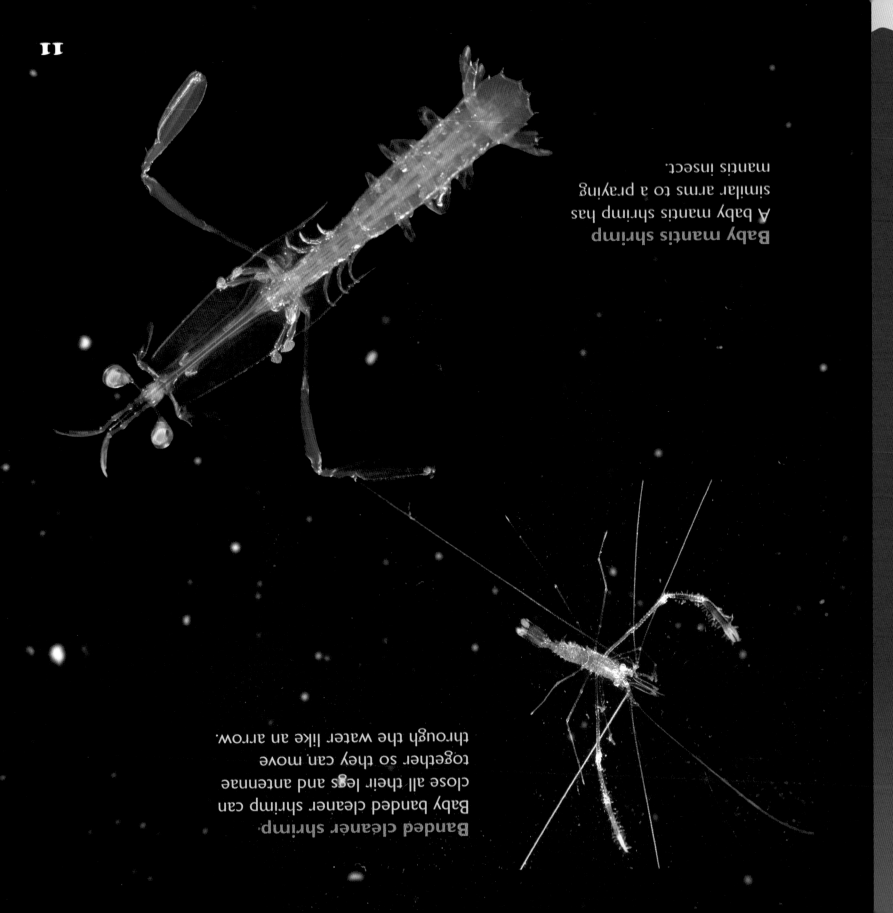

Baby mantis shrimp
A baby mantis shrimp has similar arms to a praying mantis insect.

Banded cleaner shrimp.
Baby banded cleaner shrimp can close all their legs and antennae together so they can move through the water like an arrow.

Snot and water

Jellyfish are mostly water and a substance a bit like snot, held together with a little bit of muscle. They are so delicate that many fall apart if they are removed from the water.

160ft/
48m

Scuba divers breathing air can dive this deep.

Lion's mane jellyfish
The white spots around the bell of the lion's mane jellyfish are tiny balance organs that tell the jellyfish which direction is up.

13

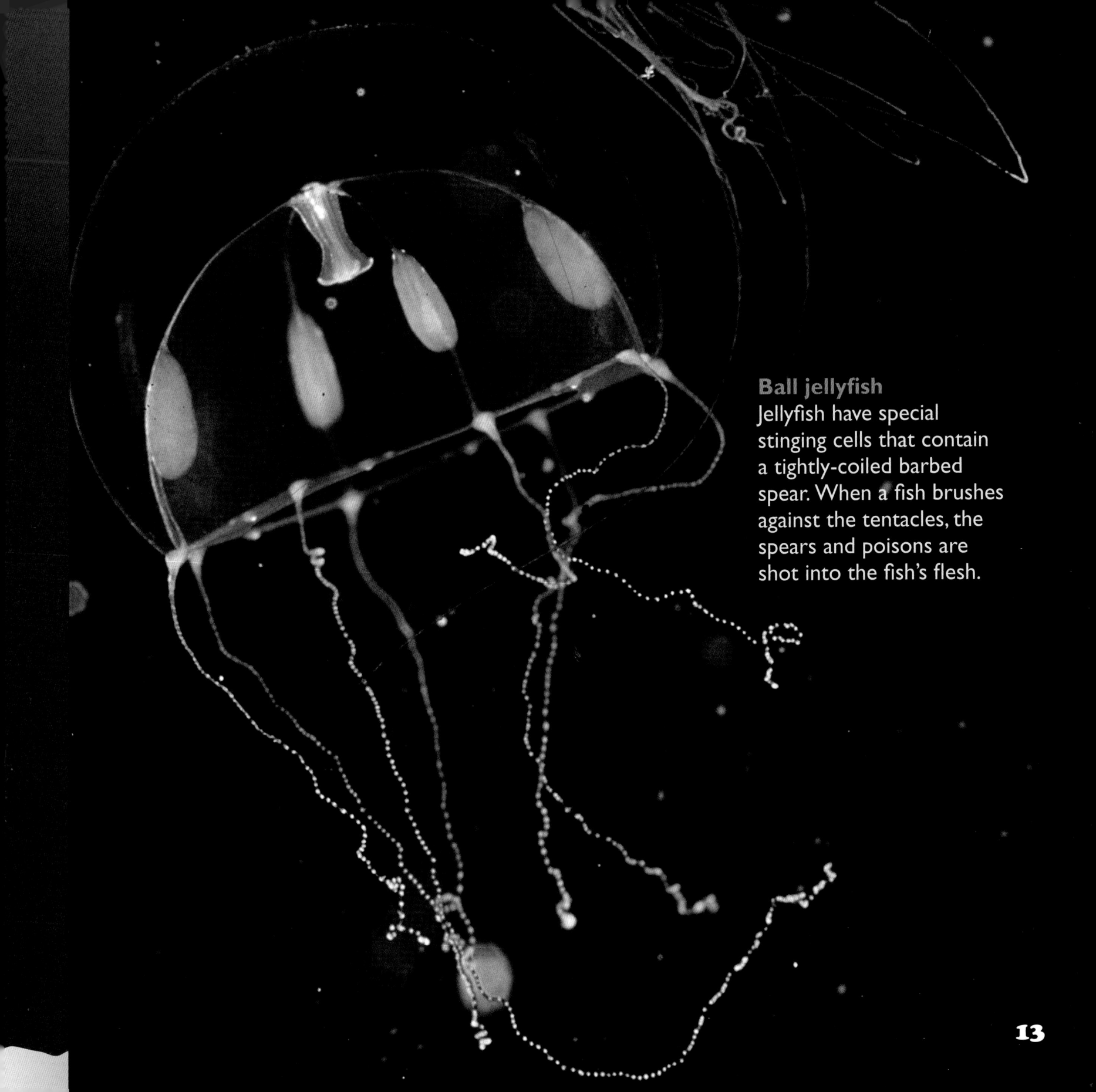

Ball jellyfish
Jellyfish have special stinging cells that contain a tightly-coiled barbed spear. When a fish brushes against the tentacles, the spears and poisons are shot into the fish's flesh.

Night risers

Many small creatures rise up from the deep every night to feed in shallow water.

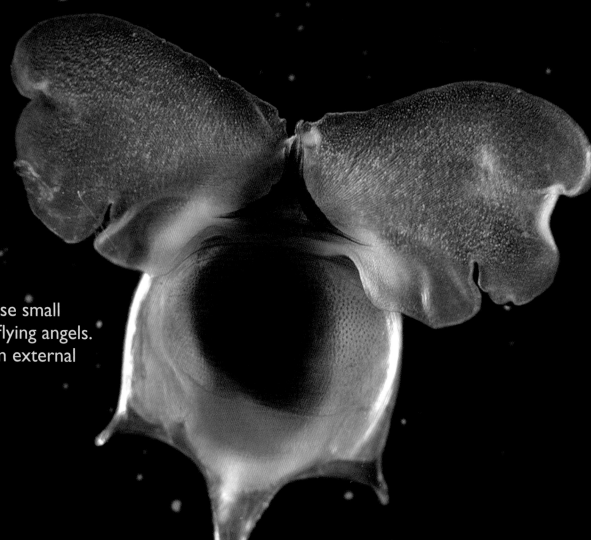

Pteropods
Pteropods (*ter-o-pods*) use small wings to swim like tiny flying angels. Some pteropods have an external shell like a turtle.

360ft/
110m

The tallest trees in the world would reach from here to the surface.

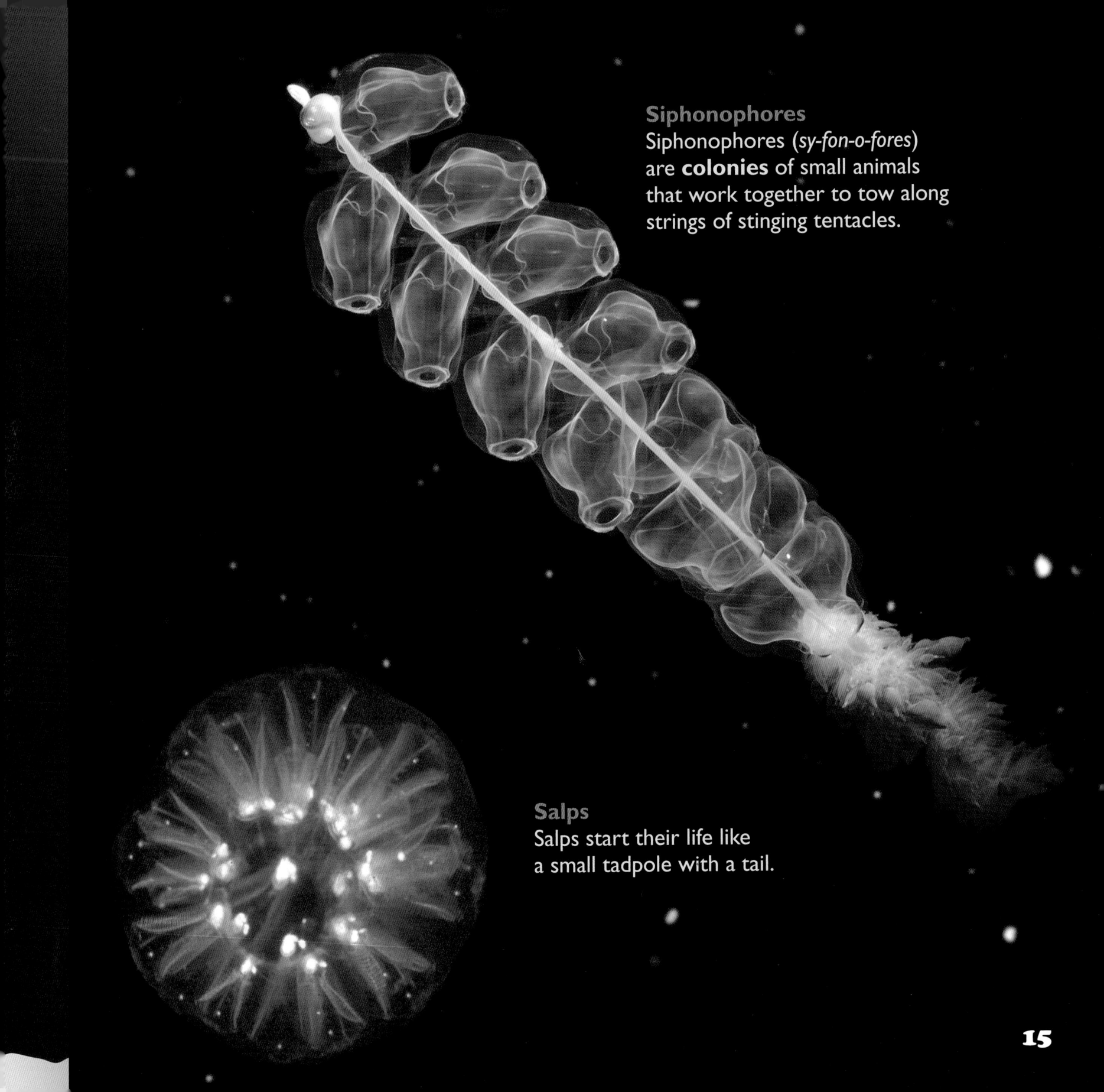

Siphonophores
Siphonophores (*sy-fon-o-fores*)
are **colonies** of small animals
that work together to tow along
strings of stinging tentacles.

Salps
Salps start their life like
a small tadpole with a tail.

Staying invisible

Below 600 feet (200 meters) is a twilight-zone of dim light. To stay hidden from predators, some animals are see-through. Others use tricks to hide their shadows from predators swimming below them.

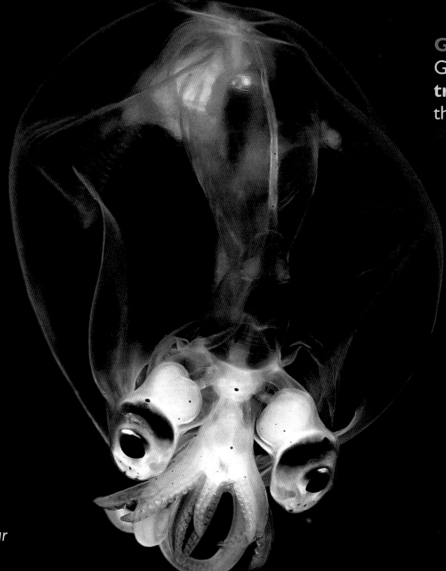

Glass squid
Glass squid are completely **transparent** except for their eyes and liver.

It's starting to get pretty dark this far down, even in the middle of the day.

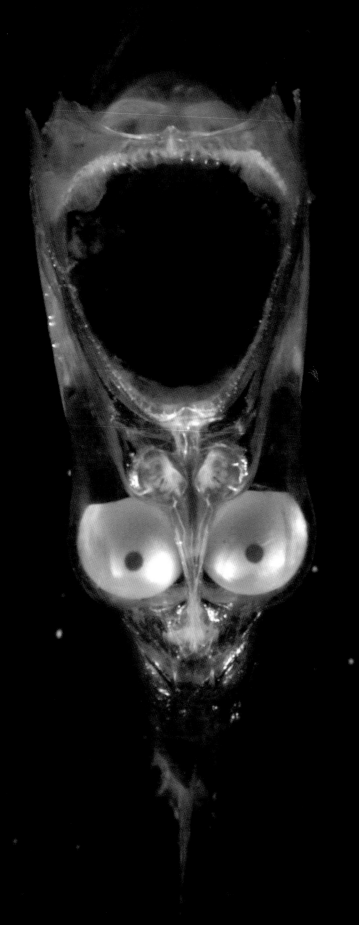

Hatchetfish

Hatchetfish are very flat and skinny, like a tomahawk. They use weak lights along their bellies to hide their skinny shadows.

Lots of teeth

It can be a long time between meals in the deep sea — sometimes months. This is why so many fish living here have big teeth. If they bite at something, they want to make sure it doesn't get away.

Dragonfish
Dragonfish even have teeth on their tongue!

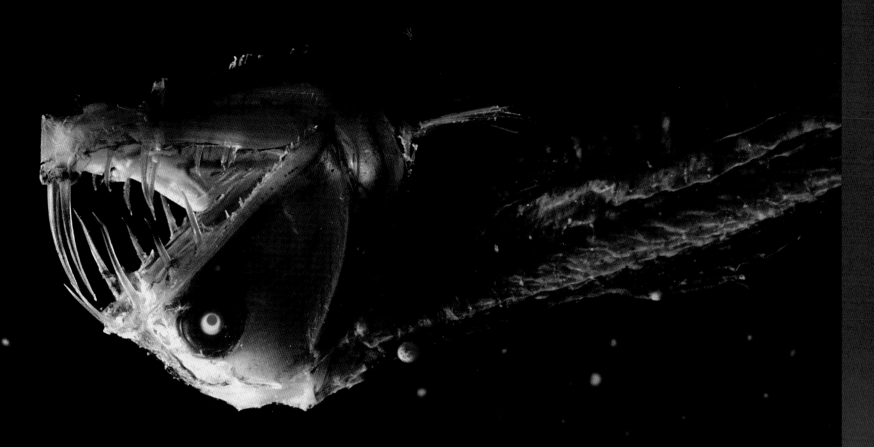

Viperfish

Viperfish can catch and swallow fish their own size. Their special rubbery neck bends back to fit in big meals. Viperfish look scary, but they are only about the length of a pencil.

Divers breathing a mix of helium and oxygen can reach here.

0.4 miles/ 0.6km

Fishing in the depths

Most fish burgers in fast-food stores around the world are made from deep-sea fish that have been dragged to the surface.

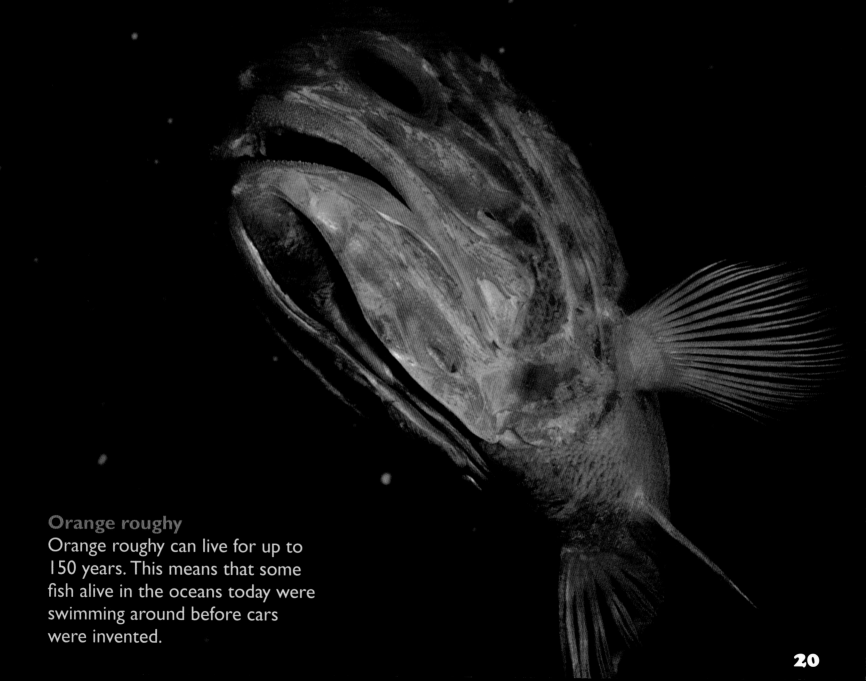

Orange roughy
Orange roughy can live for up to 150 years. This means that some fish alive in the oceans today were swimming around before cars were invented.

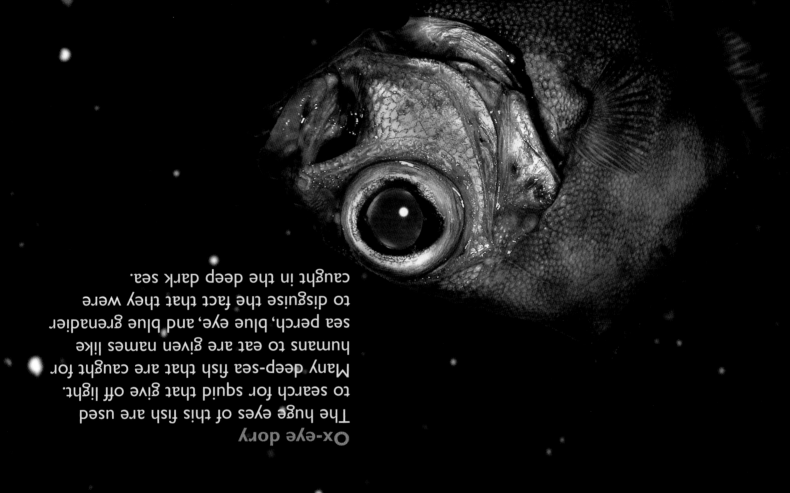

Ox-eye dory

The huge eyes of this fish are used to search for squid that give off light. Many deep-sea fish that are caught for humans to eat are given names like sea perch, blue eye, and blue grenadier to disguise the fact that they were caught in the deep dark sea.

Most deep-sea fishing nets only reach this depth.

0.5 miles/ 0.8km

Lights in the dark

Lots of deep-sea animals can make their own light.
Some use it to attract their food, others to confuse
their attackers.

Vampire squid
If attacked, the vampire squid
can squirt a cloud of glowing ink.
Bright spots in the ink can glow
for ten minutes.

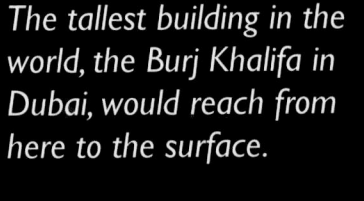

The tallest building in the world, the Burj Khalifa in Dubai, would reach from here to the surface.

0.6 miles/ 1km

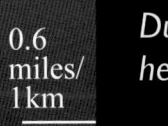

Deep-sea anglerfish

Deep-sea anglerfish have a glowing light on a rod sticking out of their face. Any creature that attacks the little light will quickly end up in the anglerfish's stomach. We don't have to be scared of deep-sea animals; this anglerfish is only about the size of a golf ball!

Finding a mate

It is difficult to find a mate in the dark. Some animals use lights, others use sound — but they have to be careful because predators might also find them.

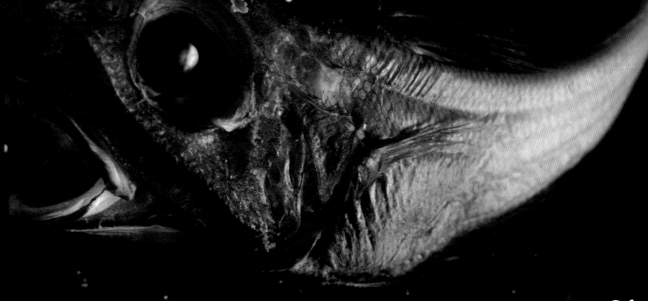

Rattail

Male rattail fishes can drum against their swim bladder, making a beat that attracts females. They have to be careful because big cods can also hear them.

Anglerfish
An anglerfish female can always find her mate, because he is hanging off her side! The male is tiny and will bite onto the female, spending the rest of his life living off her blood like a vampire.

Four Eiffel towers stacked on top of each other would reach from here to the surface.

0.9 miles/ 1.5km

Where red is black

When the light is very dim, red colors actually look like black. This is why so many animals living down this deep are bright red.

Deep-sea jellyfish
The jellyfish of the really deep sea are red, and not see-through like the jellyfish of shallower waters.

Today, this is the
deepest that submarines
containing people can go.

3.7
miles/
6km

The deepest life forms

The deepest parts of the world's oceans are in trenches — giant canyons in the seafloor. Even here, life thrives.

Sea cucumbers
The most common animals in the very deep sea are sea cucumbers. This one swims using flapping wings and a flat tail.

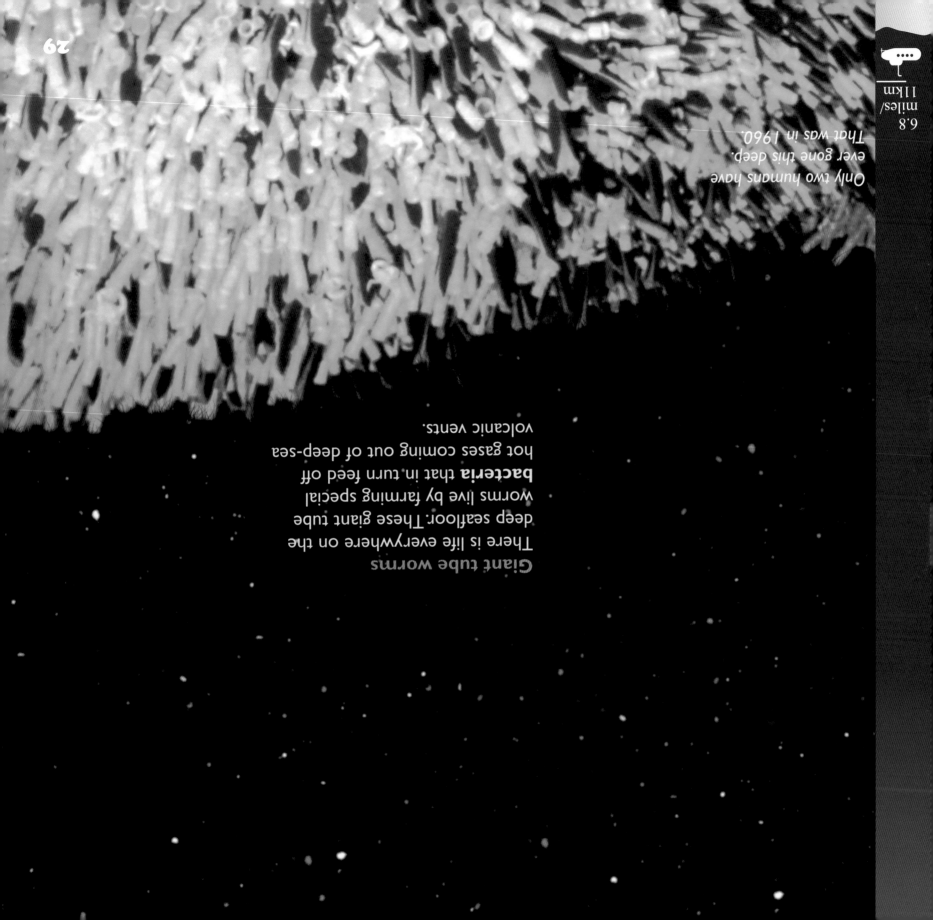

Only two humans have
ever gone this deep.
That was in 1960.

Giant tube worms
There is life everywhere on the
deep seafloor. These giant tube
worms live by farming special
bacteria that in turn feed off
hot gases coming out of deep-sea
volcanic vents.

6.8
miles/
11km

Glossary

bacteria microscopic, single-celled organisms. They are found in all living things and in all of the Earth's environments.

colony a group of organisms of the same kind that live and grow together.

plankton the collection of tiny organisms that float or drift in great numbers in water, especially near the surface. Plankton often serve as food for fishes and whales.

predator an animal that hunts and eats other animals.

prey an animal that is hunted or eaten by another animal.

Scuba stands for self-contained underwater breathing apparatus. It is a device used by divers, which consists of a mouthpiece connected to a tank of high-pressure air that is strapped to the diver's back.

transparent see-through.

water pressure the weight of the water overhead; the deeper you go, the more the water above you weighs.

Index

Further resources

Monterey Bay Aquarium Research Institute:
www.mbari.org

World Wildlife Fund for Nature:
www.worldwildlife.org

Greenpeace:
www.greenpeace.org

The Deep: The Extraordinary Creatures of the Abyss by Claire Nouvian, University of Chicago Press, 2007

This edition published in 2011 by

wild dog books

15 Gertrude Street
Fitzroy Vic 3065
Australia
+ 61 3 9419 9406
+ 61 3 9419 1214 (fax)
www.bdb.com.au
dog@bdb.com.au

wild dog books is an imprint of black dog books

Mark Norman asserts the moral right to be identified as the author of this Work.
David Paul asserts the moral right to be identified as author of this Work.

Designed by Ektavo Pty Ltd
Printed and bound in China by 1010 Printing International Pty Ltd

Distributed in the U.S.A. by
Scholastic Inc.
New York, NY 10012

ISBN: 978-1-74203-191-0 (pbk.)

10 9 8 7 6 5 4 3 2 1   11 12 13 14 15

Image Credits:
Cover: David Paul, istockphoto; Shutterstock: pp i, 2–3, 7, 31; Wikimedia Commons: p 3; Photolibrary: pp 4,
5, 6, 8, 17, 29; David Paul: pp 9 (bottom), 10–11, 12–13, 19, 20, 23, 24–25, 30, back cover; Roger Steene: p
5; Photodisk: pp 7, 8; Russ Hopcraft: p 14; Dr. Mark Norman: pp 13, 15 (bottom left), 21, 23; Kevin Raskoff
/ DeepSeaPhotography: pp 15, 27; Dave Wrobel: p 26; Peter Batson/Deep/SeaPhotography: p 16; Julian
Finn/Museum Victoria: p 18; Kim Reisenbichler: p 22; Monterey Bay Aquarium Research Institute:
p 27; Larry Madin / Woods Hole Oceanographic Instutute: p 28

FSC® is a non-profit international organisation
established to promote the responsible
management of the world's forests.